# WHEN M



# CAME IN

*Written by Alan Gibbons*
*Illustrated by Joe Rice*

Collins Educational
*An imprint of* HarperCollins*Publishers*

My father came to Liverpool
on a ship from Africa.

My mother lived round the
corner near the docks.

So what does that make me? Most of the time, it makes me happy. Today, I'm a bit sad. It's summer and it's sunny, but I'm still sad.

My dad's been at sea for weeks and I miss him. He goes where the whales can sing and the fish can fly.
I know he must miss me and mum, too, but he's a seaman and that's his life. I'm a boy of seven, and this is my life.

I'm sad about my boots, too. They've got big holes in them. Mum says there's more hole than boot. Still, there's no money for a new pair.

I see Eddie playing in the court between my front door and his.
"The sun's cracking the flags today," shouts Eddie. It isn't, but I know what he means.

Eddie's my best mate. His boots don't have holes in them, but they're a size too small now and they hurt. But he has no money for new ones either.

“Do you want to go for a walk?” he asks.
“Where?”
“Let’s go into the town,” says Eddie. We set off together, but I don’t want to walk. I want to run. My boots flap around and my feet begin to hurt. I stop to let Eddie catch up, and we stare across the Mersey together.

I squint against the sunlight and look at the sparkling waters. My dad's out there on the ocean where the world smells of salt and the floor rolls when he walks.

I'm in Liverpool where the world smells of sugar and smoke and the pavement hurts my feet when I walk.

"My boots are more trouble then they're worth," says Eddie, as he takes them off. "You're right," I agree, and kick mine off, too.

We tie our bootlaces together and hang the boots around our necks.

So that's how we walk
to town, barefoot and hot.

It’s 1901. Queen Victoria has died.
“The Queen is dead,” says Eddie. “God save the King!”
“God save my feet,” say I.
“Just think,” says Eddie. “It’s a new century, my mum told me. The twentieth century.”

"What's new about it?" I ask. "My dad still has to go away to sea, and I've still got holes in my boots."

We get a lot of funny looks from people, but I don't care. Haven't they seen anybody barefoot before? We walk past the big, grey buildings, and watch the water sparkle in the Steble fountain.

"Ow," shouts Eddie, dancing up and down.
"It's like walking on a frying pan."

"Why don't we cool off?" I ask, climbing up the side of the fountain and dangling my feet in the water.

"It's freezing!" says Eddie as he dips his feet in, too.

"You said you were too hot," I grumble. "Now you're too cold."

Eddie laughs and says, “I think it’s time to go home.”
I see two policemen watching us and nod.
“They don’t like boys putting their dirty feet in the fountain, do they?”

By the time we get home, my feet are really sore. “I need new boots,” I say, holding up my old ones.

“You’ll be lucky,” says Eddie. “There won’t be any new boots for you.”

He's wrong.
What do I see when I walk through the door of my house? A pair of shiny, new boots on the table! "But how?" I gasp.

"Can't you guess?" says Mum with a smile. "Your ship's come in."